CRIMCOMICS

SOCIAL DISORGANIZATION THEORY

KRISTA S. GEHRING

WRITER

MICHAEL R. BATISTA

ARTIST

CHERYL L. WALLACE

LETTERER

New York   Oxford

OXFORD UNIVERSITY PRESS

FOREWORD

How do you feel about your neighborhood?

Is it rich in value? Do people tend to put down roots in the community?

Do your neighbors talk to one another or meet to discuss community issues? Do they work together to solve problems or enhance community life?

Do you consider your neighborhood "safe?" Are there nearby neighborhoods you tend to avoid because you feel unsafe?

Your answers to these various questions likely highlight the idea that there are neighborhood-level dynamics behind crime. Crime is never distributed randomly across a city. Some areas are safe whereas others are relatively more crime-ridden.

The notion of a "good" versus a "bad" neighborhood even emerges in the settings of graphic novels. As one illustration, Luke Cage and Daredevil, two characters from the Marvel Universe's *Defenders*, respectively call New York's Harlem and Hell's Kitchen their homes. A reader understands these are considered traditionally "bad" neighborhoods (despite current data to the contrary). The major force behind many of these heroes' stories concerns driving out the criminal element to make their communities safer.

Along those lines, this edition of *Crim-Comics* focuses on a criminological theory that emphasizes neighborhood differences in crime rates (e.g., offenses per capita). However, the theories discussed here do not account for neighborhood differences by pointing to "good" versus "evil" people. Instead, characteristics of *neighborhood collectives* are key—factors such as *social disorganization*, *collective efficacy*, and *street culture*.

Each of these factors is defined more clearly in the comic (so I won't give away the punch lines), but I will emphasize again that they are not characteristics of individuals. Instead, they are properties of *aggregates of individuals*, or collectives (i.e., neighborhoods). Rather than "super-powered" individuals affecting neighborhood crime for good or ill, the underlying causal forces are considered to be elements and actions of a community collectivity. In this way, community-based criminological theories are inherently sociological in nature, because they look to the characteristics of the social world to explain crime. This stands in opposition to psychological, social-psychological, or biological theories that focus on individual differences in offending.

As Krista Gehring and Michael Batista's current comic describes, the community-focused tradition within American criminology was launched at the start of the twentieth century by a cadre of scholars later known as the Chicago School. This set of thinkers associated with the University of Chicago's Department of Sociology—Robert Park, Ernest Burgess, Clifford Shaw, and Henry McKay—set forth the ideas about community influence on crime that became the basis of social disorganization theory. Park, Burgess, Shaw, and McKay all come to life in the comic, as do their ideas about the sources and crime-related implications of community-level social disorganization. The theoretical paradigm that emerged from their work remains important, albeit in updated and varied forms.

Much of my own scholarship owes a debt to the Chicago School's social disorganization tradition. My interest in understanding community-level differences in crime began in the early 1990s as a PhD student in Duke University's Sociology Department. There, I studied under the mentorship of Ken Land, who is famous for, among many other things, detailing macro-level influences on crime. My studies with Ken instilled in me a great appreciation for such influences, including neighborhood effects.

After earning my doctorate, I began a career-long pursuit of understanding how patterns of crime and victimization are partly a function of community characteristics. In collaboration with a number of colleagues (e.g., Frank Cullen, Ben Feldmeyer, Terance Miethe, Barbara Warner, Marie Tillyer, Kristin Swartz, Susan McNeeley, and of course Ken Land), my scholarly work emphasizes that community rates of crime and victimization are affected by factors such as neighborhood-level socioeconomic disadvantage, the extent to which neighbors share ties and are willing to intervene in problematic behavior, and neighborhood culture.

My colleagues and I also investigate how such neighborhood characteristics moderate the effects of individual-level predictors of crime. Our work shows that the crime-inducing effects of individual risk factors can be modified—attenuated or amplified—by the characteristics of community contexts. In other words, the strength and effectiveness of a neighborhood collective can trump the effects of individual evil.

To conclude, the study of community influence on crime has been a career-related passion of mine for 25 years. Every time I walk through a city's neighborhoods for the first time, I pay attention to how neighbors relate to one another, and how effective (or not) they seem to be at thwarting neighborhood problems or modifying fellow residents' individual criminal propensities. I commend Krista and Michael for depicting this vibrant theoretical tradition in an accessible form. I hope it inspires you to understand your neighborhood and others within the context of criminological theory.

PAMELA WILCOX
University of Cincinnati

PREFACE

This is the issue I have been waiting to write. When I first began to conceptualize *Crim-Comics*, I had a lot of ideas about how we could represent social disorganization theory. I imagined Robert Park tramping about 1920s Chicago, taking in the sights of the different neighborhoods, and noticing how the development of the city had some pattern to it. I envisioned Clifford Shaw and Henry McKay, both young men from rural areas, stepping off the train in Chicago, their eyes wide when they saw the marvels of the city. The busy streets, the neighborhoods of different ethnic groups, and the sheer size of the city must have been a stark contrast to their small hometowns. Observing the sights and sounds of Chicago, then a city of about 2 million people, must have been an alien experience for them. I also had an ambitious idea for a two-page spread of a busy 1920s Chicago neighborhood: people of different ethnic backgrounds going about their business; flags of different nations in the windows of shops; new tenants moving into tenement housing; and poor individuals asking passersby for alms. I know this was a bit too ambitious, but I could *see* it, and when Mike eventually did the artwork for this issue, he translated these ideas in a way that was exactly what I wanted it to look like.

I think one of the key points of this was the realization that theory was a result of people trying to make sense of what was going on around them. Stories about the theorists embedded in their socio-historical context were what got me further invested in this theory. What resulted was a deeper understanding of social disorganization theory and my realization of its tremendous impact on criminological theory. Not only did social disorganization theory discuss crime as a community-level phenomenon, it also provided the foundation of two other branches of criminological thought: social control theories and learning theories. To me, this has always been one of the many reasons why this theory is so important.

Another reason this theory has been so impactful is its ability to explain crime from a sociological perspective at a time when much of the theorizing about criminal behavior was focused on individual explanations. For example, in 1912 Henry Goddard published his now infamous work about the Kallikak family that linked feeblemindness to criminality. Goddard was later employed at Ellis Island to administer intelligence tests (a measure of feeblemindedness) to incoming immigrants. He believed that certain ethnic groups were less intelligent than others and claimed that roughly 80 percent of the arriving Italians, Eastern European Jews, and Russians were mentally deficient. What is so remarkable about social disorganization theory is that it did not look at individual differences as popular theories at the time did; instead it focused on neighborhood characteristics that contributed to crime. Testing this theory has consistently shown that over time, crime rates in certain neighborhoods are always high, regardless of the racial or ethnic group living there. This finding illustrates the idea that criminogenic neighborhood effects can impact any group at any time. In essence, place matters.

As with any book project, *CrimComics* consumed much time and effort, perhaps more than a traditional textbook. Thinking about theories—and, in particular, trying to design a work that best conveys them in a visual medium—is fun. Still, with busy lives, finding the space in one's day to carefully research, write, illustrate, ink, and letter the pages of this work has been a source of some stress. We were fortunate, however, to have had an amazing amount of support during these times from family, friends, and Oxford University Press. We also want to acknowledge the talents of Cheryl Wallace. Cheryl's flair for lettering allowed us to get our ideas across to the readers.

The support of these and so many other individuals has made creating *CrimComics* possible and a rewarding experience for us. We would like to thank the following reviewers: Raymond Barranco, Mississippi State University; Thomas J. Chuda, Bunker Hill Community College; Ellen G. Cohn, Florida International University; Barbara Allison Crowson, Norwich University; Anna Divita, The University of North Carolina at Charlotte; and Tammy Garland, University of Tennessee, Chattanooga. We hope that this and other issues of *CrimComics* will inspire in your students a passion to learn criminological theory.

Social Disorganization Theory

WITH A FEW EXCEPTIONS, MOST EARLY CRIMINOLOGICAL THEORIES FOCUSED ON THE INDIVIDUAL.

THESE THEORIES SHARED THE ASSUMPTION THAT DISCOVERING THE CAUSES OF CRIME WOULD NOT BE FOUND BY STUDYING THE SOCIAL CONTEXT OR THE ENVIRONMENT OF INDIVIDUALS.

ONE WAY OR ANOTHER, THESE THEORIES BLAMED THE INDIVIDUAL, NOT SOCIETY, FOR THE CRIME PROBLEM.

THESE AND OTHER CIRCUMSTANCES CAUSED MILLIONS OF INDIVIDUALS TO MOVE TO URBAN CENTERS IN SEARCH OF EMPLOYMENT AND OPPORTUNITIES.

CHICAGO WAS ONE OF THE URBAN CENTERS THAT EXPERIENCED REMARKABLE GROWTH.

WHEN THE CITY WAS INCORPORATED IN 1840, IT HAD APPROXIMATELY 4,100 RESIDENTS.

BY 1890, ITS POPULATION HAD REACHED 1 MILLION...

...AND BY 1910, ITS POPULATION HAD SURPASSED 2 MILLION.

THAT'S AN INCREASE OF 1 MILLION PEOPLE IN JUST TWO DECADES!

THIS RAPID EXPANSION HAD MANY UNPLEASANT CONSEQUENCES. ALTHOUGH THOUSANDS OF PEOPLE CAME TO CHICAGO AND OTHER CITIES SEEKING WORK IN URBAN INDUSTRIES, THEY SOON FOUND THEY WOULD HAVE TO ENDURE 12-HOUR DAYS, 6 DAYS A WEEK FOR MEAGER WAGES.

FURTHERMORE, WORK CONDITIONS OFTEN JEOPARDIZED THE LABORERS' HEALTH.

LIVING CONDITIONS WERE DEPLORABLE, WITH PEOPLE PACKED INTO TENEMENT HOUSING CLOSE TO THE CENTRAL BUSINESS DISTRICT.

CRIME RATES ROSE, AND SCHOLARS BEGAN TO PROPOSE THAT GROWING UP IN THE CITY, PARTICULARLY IN THE SLUMS, IMPACTED PEOPLE'S LIVES.

THIS SHIFTED THE FOCUS OF CRIME FROM AN INDIVIDUAL PATHOLOGY TO A SOCIAL PROBLEM.

THIS CONCLUSION, MOREOVER, WAS REINFORCED BY A BROAD LIBERAL MOVEMENT THAT SPANNED A PERIOD FROM APPROXIMATELY 1890 TO 1920 CALLED THE *PROGRESSIVE ERA.*

HOUSEWIVES ALLIANCE DEMANDS PROPER INSPECTION OF MEAT

EAT NO MEAT BUY NO MEAT EAT FRESH VEGETABLES

DOWN WITH CHILD LABOR

DURING THIS TIME PERIOD, MANY DIVERSE GROUPS IN AMERICAN SOCIETY LAUNCHED EFFORTS TO REFORM OR ELIMINATE THE MANY SOCIAL PROBLEMS THAT RESULTED FROM RAPID INDUSTRIALIZATION, URBANIZATION, AND IMMIGRATION.

THE PROGRESSIVES BELIEVED THAT THE POOR WERE PUSHED BY THEIR ENVIRONMENT INTO LIVES OF CRIME.

TO COMBAT THIS, IT WAS IMPORTANT TO CHANGE THE ENVIRONMENT TO EASE THE NEGATIVE EFFECTS OF THE SLUMS.

THIS COULD BE DONE BY PROVIDING SOCIAL SERVICES LIKE SCHOOLS, CLINICS, SETTLEMENT HOUSES, RECREATIONAL FACILITIES, AND REFORMATORIES.

THESE IDEAS ABOUT THE ENVIRONMENT CAUSED REACTIONS TO ADDRESS THE PROBLEMS.

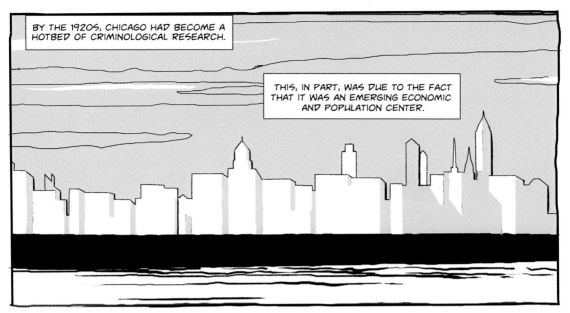

BY THE 1920S, CHICAGO HAD BECOME A HOTBED OF CRIMINOLOGICAL RESEARCH.

THIS, IN PART, WAS DUE TO THE FACT THAT IT WAS AN EMERGING ECONOMIC AND POPULATION CENTER.

ANOTHER REASON IS THAT THIS IS WHERE THE UNIVERSITY OF CHICAGO WAS LOCATED, WHICH HOUSED THE NATION'S OLDEST SOCIOLOGY PROGRAM, ESTABLISHED IN 1892.

THE FACULTY AND STUDENTS THERE WERE AFFORDED AN OPPORTUNITY TO STUDY ALL ASPECTS OF THE "URBAN LABORATORY" RIGHT OUTSIDE THEIR WINDOWS.

5

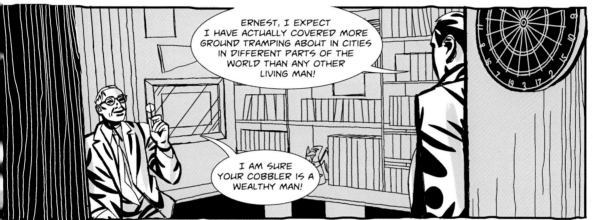

7

ROBERT PARK WAS AN URBAN SOCIOLOGIST AND IS CONSIDERED TO BE ONE OF THE MOST INFLUENTIAL FIGURES IN EARLY U.S. SOCIOLOGY.

WHEN HE WAS FACULTY AT THE UNIVERSITY OF CHICAGO, HE PLAYED A LEADING ROLE IN THE DEVELOPMENT OF THE CHICAGO SCHOOL OF CRIMINOLOGY.

TAKE YOUR SEATS, EVERYONE.

WELCOME TO "HUMAN ECOLOGY."

"ECOLOGY" IS THE STUDY OF HOW ORGANISMS ARE AFFECTED BY THEIR ENVIRONMENT. I EXPECT SOME OF YOU REMEMBER THIS TERM FROM YOUR BIOLOGY COURSES.

HUMAN ECOLOGY USES THIS CONCEPT BUT APPLIES IT TO PEOPLE. IT IS THE STUDY OF THE RELATIONSHIP BETWEEN HUMANS AND THEIR NATURAL, SOCIAL, AND PHYSICAL ENVIRONMENTS.

CITIES ARE ENVIRONMENTS THAT ARE GOVERNED BY DARWINIAN EVOLUTION, JUST LIKE WE WOULD SEE IN NATURAL ECOSYSTEMS.

BECAUSE OF THIS, I HAVE BORROWED CONCEPTS FROM NATURAL ECOLOGY, LIKE "NATURAL AREAS," "SYMBIOSIS," "INVASION," "SUCCESSION," AND "COMPETITION" TO DESCRIBE WHAT OCCURS IN DIFFERENT AREAS OF THE CITY.

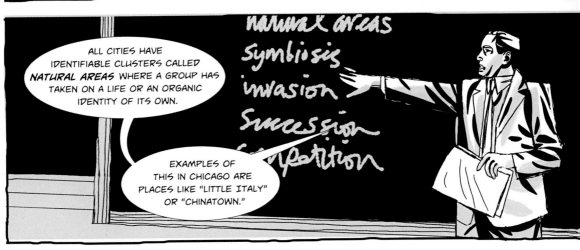

ALL CITIES HAVE IDENTIFIABLE CLUSTERS CALLED NATURAL AREAS WHERE A GROUP HAS TAKEN ON A LIFE OR AN ORGANIC IDENTITY OF ITS OWN.

EXAMPLES OF THIS IN CHICAGO ARE PLACES LIKE "LITTLE ITALY" OR "CHINATOWN."

Little Italy

"THESE NATURAL AREAS WERE CAUSED BY COMPETITION BETWEEN GROUPS IN THE CITY FOR LAND AND RESOURCES."

"THE PEOPLE IN THESE NATURAL AREAS SHARE SIMILAR SOCIAL CHARACTERISTICS BECAUSE THEY ARE SUBJECT TO THE SAME ECOLOGICAL PRESSURES."

CHINESE-AMERICAN FOOD
AIR CONDITIONED
COCKTAILS

WON KOW

THESE AREAS ENGAGE IN **COMPETITION** FOR SCARCE RESOURCES, PARTICULARLY LAND.

IN ADDITION TO THIS, **INVASION** AND **DOMINATION** OCCUR WHEN SOME AREAS INVADE AND DOMINATE AN ADJACENT AREA.

IN CITIES, IF THIS HAPPENS, THAT ADJACENT AREA MUST RECEDE OR DISAPPEAR.

"IN CHICAGO, WE CAN SEE THIS HAPPENING WHEN BUSINESSES AND FACTORIES INVADE THE RESIDENTIAL AREAS HERE."

WHEN THIS HAPPENS, IT CAUSES CHAOS AND MAKES THE RESIDENTIAL AREAS UNSTABLE.

THIS WILL INEVITABLY AFFECT THE ORGANISMS-- THE HUMANS--WHO LIVE THERE.

LATER...

ERNEST BURGESS WAS AN URBAN SOCIOLOGIST AND A FACULTY MEMBER AT THE UNIVERSITY OF CHICAGO.

HIS GROUNDBREAKING RESEARCH, IN COLLABORATION WITH HIS COLLEAGUE ROBERT PARK, PROVIDED THE FOUNDATION FOR THE *CHICAGO SCHOOL OF CRIMINOLOGY.*

SORRY I'M LATE.

OH, NO PROBLEM, FRIEND!

BUT WAIT, BEFORE YOU SIT DOWN, I WANT TO SHOW YOU WHAT I'VE BEEN WORKING ON!

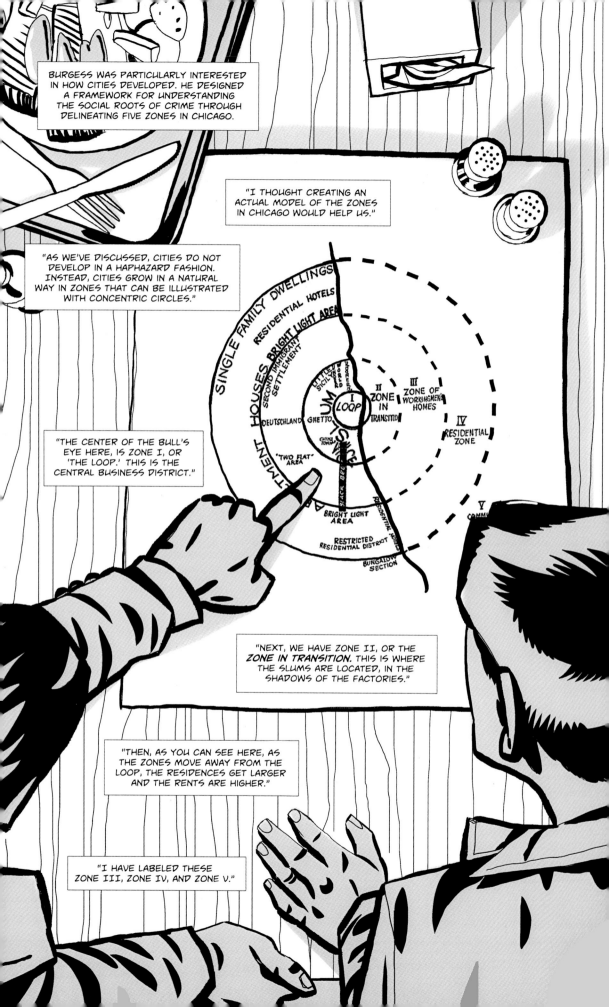

THE ZONE IN TRANSITION IS THE MOST PROBLEMATIC. THIS AREA IS IN CONSTANT FLUX.

NO ONE WANTS TO LIVE HERE, BUT THIS IS TYPICALLY THE FIRST PLACE PEOPLE GO WHEN THEY ARRIVE IN THE CITY.

YES, THIS IS WHERE IMMIGRANTS AND MIGRANTS WHO DO NOT HAVE THE MONEY TO LIVE ANYWHERE ELSE TEND TO GO.

AND THERE IS THE CONSTANT PUSH, OR INVASION, OF THE BUSINESS DISTRICT THAT CAUSES THE RESIDENTS TO BE CONTINUOUSLY DISPLACED.

NOT TO MENTION NO ONE REALLY WANTS TO LIVE THERE. THEY ARE IN CLOSE TO THE FACTORIES AND THE AIR IS POLLUTED...

THOSE PHENOMENA MAKE THE FAMILY AND COMMUNAL TIES IN THE ZONE IN TRANSITION WEAK. SOCIAL INSTITUTIONS ARE NOT ABLE TO CONTROL THE RESIDENTS.

BECAUSE OF THIS, THERE ARE HIGHER RATES OF MANY SOCIAL PATHOLOGIES, INCLUDING CRIME, IN THE ZONE IN TRANSITION.

YES, AND AS WE MOVE FARTHER AWAY FROM DOWNTOWN, CRIME AND OTHER SOCIAL MALADIES DECREASE.

THIS LOOKS FANTASTIC, ERNEST! YOU HAVE REALLY BROUGHT *CONCENTRIC ZONE THEORY* TO LIFE!

SHAW AND MCKAY PLOTTED THE RESIDENCES OF OFFICIAL DELINQUENTS ON MAPS OF CHICAGO.

111 SOUTH MICHIGAN AVENUE.

108 NORTH STATE STREET.

"SPOT MAPS," WITH ONE SPOT PER DELINQUENCY CASE, SHOWED THE ACTUAL RESIDENTIAL DISTRIBUTION OF THE DELINQUENTS.

OTHER MAPS WERE MADE, SUCH AS "ZONE MAPS," THAT SHOWED THE DELINQUENCY RATES IN CONCENTRIC ZONES DRAWN AT ONE-MILE INTERVALS FROM THE CITY CENTER.

THESE CALCULATIONS LED TO A STARTLING DISCOVERY...

I'VE CALCULATED THE DELINQUENCY RATES IN THESE AREAS AND IT APPEARS THAT THEY ARE HIGHEST IN ZONE I AND ZONE II, THE ZONE IN TRANSITION, JUST AS THE THEORY PREDICTED!

FURTHERMORE, RATES DECREASED AS WE MOVE AWAY FROM THE CENTRAL BUSINESS DISTRICT TO MORE AFFLUENT AREAS OF THE CITY.

I ALSO CALCULATED RATES FOR DIFFERENT TIME PERIODS: 1900-1906, 1917-1923, AND 1927-1933.

AND?

IT APPEARS THAT THESE AREAS HAVE HIGH DELINQUENCY RATES REGARDLESS OF WHO LIVES THERE!

SEVERAL YEARS LATER, TWO FARM BOYS TRAVELED TO CHICAGO TO PURSUE A DOCTORAL DEGREE IN SOCIOLOGY AT THE UNIVERSITY OF CHICAGO.

THEY WERE EXPOSED TO THESE IDEAS ABOUT THE CITY AND ITS INFLUENCE ON ITS RESIDENTS.

CHICAGO WAS DRAMATICALLY DIFFERENT FROM THE COMMUNITIES THEY CAME FROM.

CLIFFORD SHAW WAS FROM A SMALL TOWN IN INDIANA. HE WAS TALKATIVE, FRIENDLY, PERSONABLE, PERSUASIVE, AND ENERGETIC.

HENRY MCKAY WAS BORN ON A 300-ACRE FARM IN SOUTH DAKOTA. HE WAS POLITE, KIND, AND THOUGHTFUL. A GENTLEMAN IN EVERY DEFINITION OF THE TERM.

ALTHOUGH SHAW AND MCKAY DIDN'T FINISH THEIR DOCTORAL STUDIES, THEY USED WHAT THEY LEARNED FROM THEIR COURSES WHEN THEY BOTH BECAME EMPLOYED AT THE INSTITUTE FOR JUVENILE RESEARCH NEAR THE CHICAGO LOOP.

AS DIRECTOR OF THAT INSTITUTE, SHAW WAS MORE OF AN ACTIVIST. HE "RELATED" TO THE DELINQUENTS AND WAS ABLE TO OBTAIN THEIR LIFE STORIES.

HE WAS AN EMOTIONAL PRACTITIONER.

HENRY! YOU WON'T BELIEVE WHAT STANLEY TOLD ME TODAY!

MCKAY, ON THE OTHER HAND, WAS A QUIET STATISTICIAN.

YOU DO HAVE A KNACK WITH THOSE BOYS, CLIFF. THEY SEEM TO TELL YOU EVERYTHING.

IT'S REALLY QUITE EXTRAORDINARY! THROUGH MY INTERVIEWS WITH HIM AND OTHER DELINQUENTS, I'M FINDING THAT ONE OF THE MAIN REASONS FOR THEIR CRIMINAL INVOLVEMENT IS BECAUSE THEY LEARNED IT FROM OLDER DELINQUENTS AND GANG MEMBERS.

MORE MATERIAL FOR YOUR BOOK, MY FRIEND!

SHAW WROTE *THE JACK-ROLLER: A DELINQUENT BOY'S OWN STORY* IN 1930. IT DETAILED THE LIFE HISTORY OF A JUVENILE DELINQUENT IN CHICAGO.

THIS AND OTHER AUTOBIOGRAPHIES OF DELINQUENTS COLLECTED AT THE INSTITUTE HELPED SHAW AND MCKAY UNDERSTAND DELINQUENCY IN URBAN AREAS.

IN THE EARLY 1930S, SHAW INITIATED THE **CHICAGO AREA PROJECT (CAP)** IN THREE HIGH-DELINQUENCY AREAS IN CHICAGO.

SINCE SHAW BELIEVED THAT DELINQUENCY WAS A RESULT OF A NEIGHBORHOOD'S SOCIAL DISORGANIZATION AND DETERIORATION, CAP'S GOAL WAS TO STOP DELINQUENCY BY CALLING ON LOCALS TO ACTIVELY ENGAGE IN COMMUNITY SELF-DEVELOPMENT.

CAP IDENTIFIED COMMUNITY LEADERS AND SUPPORTED THEIR GRASSROOTS EFFORTS TO MOBILIZE RESIDENTS TO TAKE RESPONSIBILITY FOR GUIDING THE YOUNG PEOPLE IN THEIR NEIGHBORHOODS AND TO SOLVE NEIGHBORHOOD-SPECIFIC ISSUES.

THE AIM WAS TO "STIMULATE" COMMUNITY ORGANIZATION AND TO "SPARK" THE LATENT POTENTIAL FOR COMMUNITY CONTROL.

THE PROGRAM IS CONSIDERED TO BE AMERICA'S FIRST COMMUNITY-BASED DELINQUENCY PREVENTION PROGRAM AND IS STILL IN EXISTENCE TODAY.

IDEAS CAUSE REACTIONS.

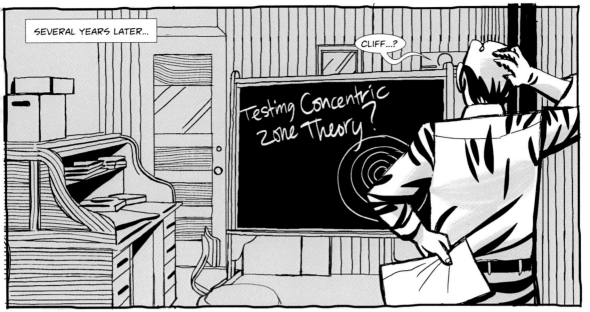

SHAW AND MCKAY PLOTTED THE RESIDENCES OF OFFICIAL DELINQUENTS ON MAPS OF CHICAGO.

111 SOUTH MICHIGAN AVENUE.

108 NORTH STATE STREET.

"SPOT MAPS," WITH ONE SPOT PER DELINQUENCY CASE, SHOWED THE ACTUAL RESIDENTIAL DISTRIBUTION OF THE DELINQUENTS.

OTHER MAPS WERE MADE, SUCH AS "ZONE MAPS," THAT SHOWED THE DELINQUENCY RATES IN CONCENTRIC ZONES DRAWN AT ONE-MILE INTERVALS FROM THE CITY CENTER.

THESE CALCULATIONS LED TO A STARTLING DISCOVERY...

I'VE CALCULATED THE DELINQUENCY RATES IN THESE AREAS AND IT APPEARS THAT THEY ARE HIGHEST IN ZONE I AND ZONE II, THE ZONE IN TRANSITION, JUST AS THE THEORY PREDICTED!

FURTHERMORE, RATES DECREASED AS WE MOVE AWAY FROM THE CENTRAL BUSINESS DISTRICT TO MORE AFFLUENT AREAS OF THE CITY.

I ALSO CALCULATED RATES FOR DIFFERENT TIME PERIODS: 1900-1906, 1917-1923, AND 1927-1933.

AND?

IT APPEARS THAT THESE AREAS HAVE HIGH DELINQUENCY RATES *REGARDLESS OF WHO LIVES THERE!*

THESE AREAS/NEIGHBORHOODS WERE CHARACTERIZED BY THREE THINGS:

1) LOW SOCIOECONOMIC STATUS. THERE ARE INADEQUATE RESOURCES IN THESE AREAS AND THE RESIDENTS LIVE IN POVERTY.

2) ETHNIC HETEROGENEITY. DIFFERENT RACIAL AND ETHNIC GROUPS LIVE TOGETHER IN THESE AREAS, AND DIFFERENCES IN CULTURE AND LANGUAGE CREATE BARRIERS. PEOPLE ISOLATE THEMSELVES, AVOID MEANINGFUL INTERACTION, AND DON'T HAVE MUCH IN COMMON.

3) RESIDENTIAL INSTABILITY. THERE IS CONSTANT POPULATION TURNOVER. RESIDENTS MOVE FREQUENTLY OR ARE LOOKING TO MOVE OUT OF THESE AREAS.

BECAUSE OF THESE STRUCTURAL VARIABLES (I.E., CHARACTERISTICS OF AN ENVIRONMENT), CERTAIN AREAS OF THE CITY HAD HIGH CRIME RATES NO MATTER WHO LIVED THERE.

THIS LED SHAW AND MCKAY TO CONCLUDE THAT THE ORGANIZATION OF A NEIGHBORHOOD WAS KEY IN PROMOTING OR PREVENTING DELINQUENCY.

THESE NEIGHBORHOODS EXPERIENCED *SOCIAL DISORGANIZATION.*

LEFT TO THEIR OWN DEVICES, SLUM YOUTHS WERE FREED FROM THE TYPE OF SOCIAL CONTROLS FOUND IN MORE AFFLUENT AREAS.

NO GUIDING FORCE EXISTED TO STOP THEM FROM SEEKING EXCITEMENT AND ENGAGING IN DELINQUENT ACTS IN THE STREETS OF THE CITY.

IN THESE SOCIALLY DISORGANIZED NEIGHBORHOODS, THE CORE INSTITUTIONS THAT HELP KEEP KIDS IN LINE ARE WEAK.

EXAMPLES OF INSTITUTIONS THAT HELP WITH INFORMAL SOCIAL CONTROL INCLUDE FAMILY, SCHOOLS, AND CHURCHES.

WHEN THESE INFORMAL CONTROLS BREAK DOWN, TEENS RUN AMOK. THEREFORE, THE *LACK OF INFORMAL SOCIAL CONTROL* IN THESE NEIGHBORHOODS CONTRIBUTES TO DELINQUENCY.

SHAW AND MCKAY ALSO INTEGRATED WHAT THEY LEARNED FROM THE LIFE HISTORIES OF YOUTHS IN THESE NEIGHBORHOODS AND PROPOSED THAT SOCIALLY DISORGANIZED AREAS WERE ALSO CHARACTERIZED BY *CULTURAL TRANSMISSION.*

GENERATIONS OF DELINQUENTS WOULD PASS ON ANTISOCIAL ATTITUDES AND VALUES TO THE NEXT, THUS PRODUCING AND SUSTAINING "CRIMINAL TRADITIONS" IN THESE NEIGHBORHOODS.

SPAK

THAT IS, DELINQUENTS LEARNED FROM ONE ANOTHER ANTISOCIAL BEHAVIORS AND THE ATTITUDES THAT SUPPORTED THEM.

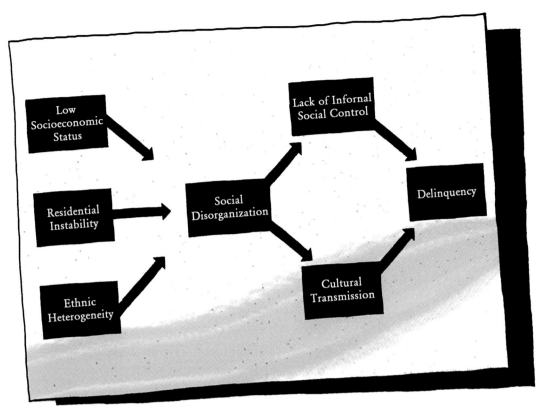

SHAW AND MCKAY'S *SOCIAL DISORGANIZATION THEORY* EXPLAINED HIGH CRIME RATES IN CITY NEIGHBORHOODS. THEY PRESENTED THEIR RESEARCH IN THEIR BOOK *JUVENILE DELINQUENCY AND URBAN AREAS* (1942). THESE IDEAS HAVE BECOME THE FOUNDATION OF TWO CRIMINOLOGICAL PERSPECTIVES THAT ARE IMPORTANT TODAY. ON THE ONE HAND, SHAW AND MCKAY'S PREMISE THAT WEAKENING SOCIAL CONTROLS PERMIT DELINQUENCY TO TAKE PLACE IS AN EARLY VERSION OF WHAT WAS LATER TO BECOME CONTROL THEORIES. ON THE OTHER HAND, THE IDEA THAT CRIMINAL BEHAVIOR OCCURS AS A RESULT OF CULTURAL TRANSMISSION GAVE RISE TO LEARNING THEORIES. FOLLOW-UP STUDIES OF CHICAGO CONTINUED TO FIND THE SAME PATTERN OVER TIME, AND STUDIES OF OTHER CITIES FOUND SIMILAR CONCENTRIC ZONE PATTERNS AS WELL.

ALBANY, NEW YORK. 1979.

AS WE HAVE SEEN, STUDENTS ARE OFTEN INFLUENCED BY THE IDEAS THEY ARE EXPOSED TO IN CLASS.

WHILE A GRADUATE STUDENT AT THE UNIVERSITY AT ALBANY-SUNY, *ROBERT SAMPSON* ENROLLED IN A SEMINAR TAUGHT BY TRAVIS HIRSCHI.*

HIRSCHI WAS AN ADVOCATE OF CONTROL THEORY. HE INTRODUCED HIS STUDENTS TO WORKS THAT SUPPORTED THIS VIEWPOINT.

*MORE ON TRAVIS HIRSCHI IN *CRIMCOMICS: SOCIAL CONTROL THEORIES!*

A CLOSE READING OF RUTH KORNHAUSER'S BOOK PROVIDED SAMPSON WITH AN "INTELLECTUAL JOLT."

SOCIAL SOURCES OF DELINQUENCY
Ruth R. Kornhauser

ONE FOCUS OF THIS TEXT WAS THE DISCUSSION OF A "PURE CONTROL VERSION OF SOCIAL DISORGANIZATION THEORY."

THE FOCUS WAS THE INABILITY OF A COMMUNITY TO REALIZE THE COMMON VALUES OF ITS RESIDENTS TO MAINTAIN EFFECTIVE SOCIAL CONTROLS.

HEY, HAVE YOU READ KORNHAUSER YET? I'M INTRIGUED BY HOW SHE DEFINES SOCIAL DISORGANIZATION.

IT'S LIKE HIRSCHI'S CONTROL THEORY BUT AT THE *MACRO-LEVEL!** CAN YOU DIG IT?

THE CONCEPT OF CONTROL AT THE MACRO-LEVEL RESONATED WITH SAMPSON, AND HE, ALONG WITH OTHERS, BEGAN TO VIEW SOCIAL DISORGANIZATION THEORY AS A SYSTEMIC MODEL THAT FOCUSED ON INFORMAL SOCIAL CONTROL.

*MACRO-LEVEL FOCUSES ON GROUPS AND EXPLAINS CRIME IN THE AGGREGATE.

UNIVERSITY OF ILLINOIS, CHAMPAIGN, APPROXIMATELY 10 YEARS LATER...

SAMPSON CONTINUED TO STUDY AND DEVELOP SOCIAL DISORGANIZATION THEORY AFTER GRADUATE SCHOOL.

HEY FRIEND! HEY YEAH, IT'S GOOD TO HEAR YOUR VOICE TOO... I HOPE WISCONSIN IS TREATING YOU WELL...

HEY, REMEMBER ALL THOSE NIGHTS WE STAYED UP TALKING ABOUT KORNHAUSER? I'VE GOT AN IDEA FOR A PUBLICATION AND WANTED TO KNOW IF YOU WERE INTERESTED IN BEING A CO-AUTHOR...

SAMPSON, WITH HIS COLLEAGUE W. BYRON GROVES, USED THE BRITISH CRIME SURVEY TO TEST VARIABLES IN THE DATASET THEY BELIEVED REPRESENTED "SOCIAL DISORGANIZATION."

THEY DISCOVERED THAT COMMUNITIES CHARACTERIZED BY UNSUPERVISED TEENAGERS, LIMITED FRIENDSHIP NETWORKS, AND LITTLE PARTICIPATION IN LOCAL ORGANIZATIONS HAD HIGHER CRIME RATES.

THIS PUBLICATION WAS A CLASSIC TEST OF SHAW AND MCKAY'S WORK (SAMPSON & GROVES, 1989).

INTERESTINGLY ENOUGH, IN THE EARLY 1990S, SAMPSON SECURED A FACULTY POSITION AT THE UNIVERSITY OF CHICAGO. WHILE THERE, HE CONTINUED TO EXPLORE SOCIAL DISORGANIZATION THEORY, AND WITH SOME COLLEAGUES (STEVEN RAUDENBUSH AND FELTON EARLS) PROPOSED AN EXCITING NEW RECONCEPTUALIZATION OF THE SOCIAL DISORGANIZATION FRAMEWORK THEY CALLED **COLLECTIVE EFFICACY.**

FRED? WHAT ARE YOU DOING?

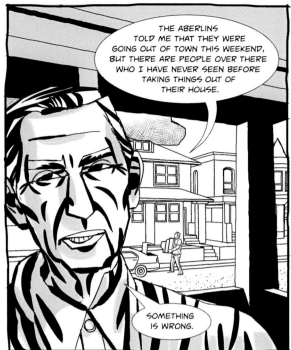

THE ABERLINS TOLD ME THAT THEY WERE GOING OUT OF TOWN THIS WEEKEND, BUT THERE ARE PEOPLE OVER THERE WHO I HAVE NEVER SEEN BEFORE TAKING THINGS OUT OF THEIR HOUSE.

SOMETHING IS WRONG.

SARA, I'M CALLING THE POLICE.

COLLECTIVE EFFICACY IS A PHENOMENON THAT OCCURS IN COMMUNITIES WHERE THERE IS MUTUAL TRUST AND SUPPORT COUPLED WITH SHARED EXPECTATIONS FOR SOCIAL CONTROL, AND THE WILLINGNESS TO TAKE ACTION AND INTERVENE FOR THE COMMON GOOD.

IT ADDED THE ELEMENT OF PURPOSIVE ACTION TO THE CONCEPT OF CONTROL.

ELSEWHERE...

SAMPSON'S RESEARCH DISCOVERED THAT NEIGHBORHOODS WITH HIGH LEVELS OF COLLECTIVE EFFICACY HAVE LOWER CRIME RATES...

ARCHIE? WHAT ARE YOU DOING?

...WHILE NEIGHBORHOODS WITH WEAK COLLECTIVE EFFICACY DO NOT HAVE THE SOCIAL CAPITAL TO ASSERT INFORMAL SOCIAL CONTROLS AND KEEP THE NEIGHBORHOOD SAFE. CRIME RATES IN THESE NEIGHBORHOODS ARE HIGHER.

NOTHING, EDITH.

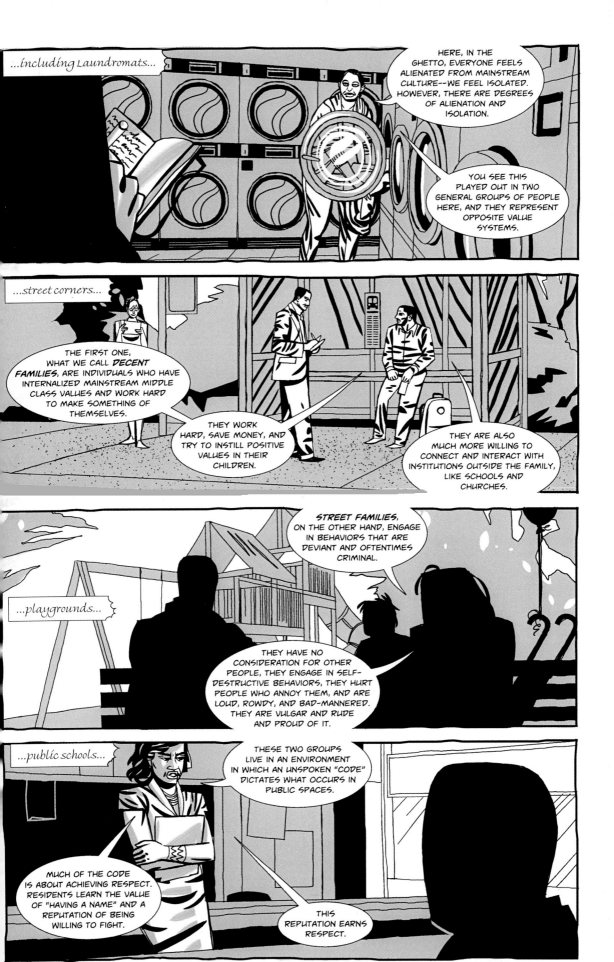

THIS ISSUE BEGAN WITH A DISCUSSION OF THE HISTORICAL CONTEXT IN WHICH CITIES IN THE UNITED STATES HAD EXPERIENCED UNPRECEDENTED GROWTH. THIS GROWTH ALSO BROUGHT AN INCREASE IN CRIME. THE CITY OF CHICAGO WAS A PRIME EXAMPLE OF HOW IMMIGRATION, URBANIZATION, AND INDUSTRIALIZATION CHANGED URBAN LANDSCAPES AND CAUSED CERTAIN AREAS TO HAVE HIGHER CRIME RATES THAN OTHERS. ROBERT PARK, ONE OF THE MOST INFLUENTIAL AMERICAN SOCIOLOGISTS, BORROWED CONCEPTS FROM BIOLOGY TO EXPLAIN HOW CITIES AFFECTED RESIDENTS. THIS WAS REFERRED TO AS HUMAN ECOLOGY. PARK, ALONG WITH HIS COLLEAGUE ERNEST BURGESS, DEVELOPED A FRAMEWORK FOR UNDERSTANDING THE SOCIAL ROOTS OF CRIME THROUGH DELINEATING FIVE ZONES IN CHICAGO. THIS WAS REFERRED TO AS CONCENTRIC ZONE THEORY.

CLIFFORD SHAW AND HENRY MCKAY WERE EXPOSED TO THESE IDEAS WHEN THEY PURSUED THEIR DOCTORAL DEGREES AT THE UNIVERSITY OF CHICAGO. THIS LED TO MAJOR CONTRIBUTIONS THAT CAN BE DIVIDED INTO THREE MAIN AREAS: A) COLLECTION OF AUTOBIOGRAPHIES OF JUVENILE DELINQUENTS, B) CREATION OF A DELINQUENCY PROGRAM KNOWN AS THE CHICAGO AREA PROJECT (CAP), AND C) RESEARCH ON THE GEOGRAPHICAL DISTRIBUTION OF DELINQUENTS. THEIR RESEARCH LED TO THE DEVELOPMENT OF SOCIAL DISORGANIZATION THEORY. THIS THEORY PROPOSED THAT NEIGHBORHOODS WITH LOW SOCIOECONOMIC STATUS, ETHNIC HETEROGENEITY, AND RESIDENTIAL INSTABILITY WOULD BE SOCIALLY DISORGANIZED. THIS DISORGANIZATION MANIFESTS ITSELF AS A LACK OF INFORMAL SOCIAL CONTROL AND THE CULTURAL TRANSMISSION OF CRIMINAL TRADITIONS. ROBERT SAMPSON CONTINUED TO DEVELOP THIS THEORY AND RECONCEPTUALIZED IT WITH THE CONCEPT OF COLLECTIVE EFFICACY. IN THE MID-1990S, THERE WAS A RENEWED INTEREST IN THE CULTURAL DIMENSION OF THIS THEORY. ELIJAH ANDERSON'S RESEARCH DISCOVERED THE CODE OF THE STREETS, A SET OF UNSPOKEN LAWS THAT GOVERNED BEHAVIOR IN PUBLIC SPACES IN THESE DISORGANIZED NEIGHBORHOODS. THIS ISSUE ILLUSTRATED HOW NEIGHBORHOODS POSSESS RELATIVELY ENDURING FEATURES THAT TRANSCEND THE INDIVIDUAL CHARACTERISTICS OF THEIR RESIDENTS AND HOW THESE FEATURES AFFECT CRIME RATES.

Key Terms

Progressive Era
Robert Park
Chicago School of Criminology
Human Ecology
Natural Areas
Competition
Invasion
Domination
Ernest Burgess
Chicago School of Criminology
Zone in Transition
Concentric Zone Theory
Clifford Shaw
Henry McKay
Chicago Area Project (CAP)
Low Socioeconomic Status
Ethnic Heterogeneity
Residential Instability
Social Disorganization
Lack of Informal Social Control
Cultural Transmission
Social Disorganization Theory
Robert Sampson
Macro-Level
Collective Efficacy
Elijah Anderson
Decent Families
Street Families
Code of the Street

Discussion Questions

What does it mean to say that a community is "socially disorganized"? Why is crime less likely to occur in an organized community?

Although written several decades ago, how might Shaw and McKay's theory help explain the occurrence of crime in today's inner-city communities?

Think back to your childhood. Was the level of collective efficacy high or low in your neighborhood? Give examples of when examples of collective efficacy were or were not activated to deal with public disorder or troublesome behaviors.

Describe the central values and norms (or rules) that form the "code of the streets." Why do individuals who oppose the code of the streets conform to its rules on occasion?

Suggested Readings

Anderson, E. (1999). *Code of the street: Decency, violence, and the moral life of the inner city.* New York: W. W. Norton.

Cullen, F. T., Agnew, R., & Wilcox, P. (2014). *Criminological theory: Past to present* (5th ed.). New York: Oxford University Press.

Lilly, J. R., Cullen, F. T., & Ball, R. (2011). *Criminological theory: Context and consequences* (5th ed.). Los Angeles: Sage Publications.

Park, R., & Burgess, E. (1925). *The city*. Chicago: University of Chicago Press.

Sampson, R. (2011). Communities and crime revisited: Intellectual trajectory of a Chicago school education. In F. T. Cullen et al. (Eds.), *The origins of American criminology* (pp. 63–85). New Brunswick: Transaction Publishers.

Sampson, R., & Groves, W. (1989). Community structure and crime: Testing social disorganization theory. *American Journal of Sociology*, 94, 774–802.

Sampson, R., Raudenbush, S., & Earls, F. (1997). Neighborhoods and violent crime: A multilevel study of collective efficacy. *Science*, 277 (August 15), 916–924.

Shaw, C., & McKay, H. (1942). *Juvenile delinquency and urban areas*. Chicago: University of Chicago Press.

Snodgrass, J. (2011). Clifford Shaw and Henry McKay: Chicago criminologists. In F. T. Cullen et al. (Eds.), *The origins of American criminology* (pp. 17–35). New Brunswick: Transaction Publishers.